The Man who met Jesus at Bethesda

JOHN 5:1-14 FOR CHILDREN

Written by Neal A. Boehlke
Illustrated by Fred Stout and Herb Halpern Productions

ARCH Books

Copyright © 1981 CONCORDIA PUBLISHING HOUSE
ST. LOUIS, MISSOURI
MANUFACTURED IN THE UNITED STATES OF AMERICA
ISBN 0-570-06143-1

It was so very long ago,
In Palestine we're told,
There lived a little boy who was,
As boys are, strong and bold.

He was a very happy boy
Who loved to run and play.
He had a lot of little friends
He played with every day.

2

His parents were good people, too.
They taught him in God's way.
Together they would read God's Word
And every day would pray.

One morning all their lives were changed;
The boy would not awake.
He had a fever so severe
They could not make it break.

His mother tried to cool him off
The best way she knew how.
She in cold water dipped a sponge
And placed it on his brow.

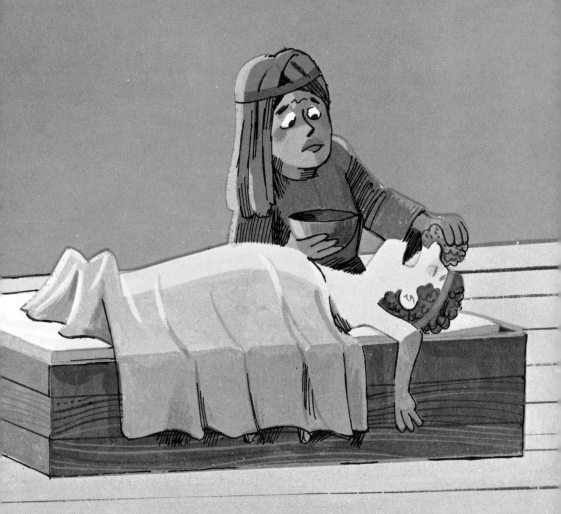

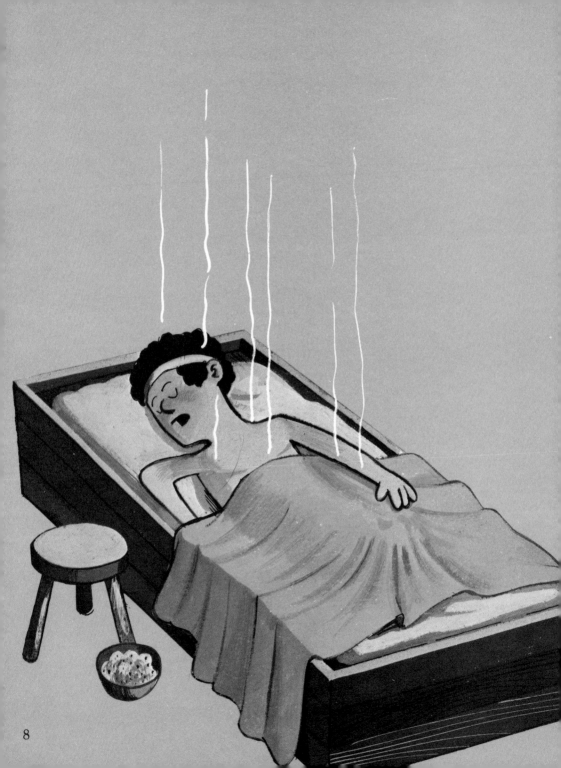

His parents prayed to God above
To spare their only son.
But in their prayers they also said,
"Your will, not ours, be done."

God responded to their prayers;
The fever soon went down.
Their son felt better once again;
He smiled and looked around.

His parents fell upon their knees
To thank their God and Lord
For not allowing him to die,
For strength to him restored.

But God in His great wisdom
Did not *all* his strength restore.
They realized soon, though he was well,
He could move his legs no more.

They still were thankful for their son,
Although he could not walk.
He had his hands, he had his mind,
He still could laugh and talk.

His parents took good care of him;
They'd carry him about.
They all still had true faith in God;
His love they did not doubt.

As years went by the young boy grew;
He was no longer small.
His mother thought, *If he could stand,*
He would be very tall.

His parents too were growing old,
Their hair had now turned gray.
To care for their own son they found
It harder with each day.

Their friends and neighbors noticed too
How hard it was for them;
So they suggested that they take
Him to Jerusalem.

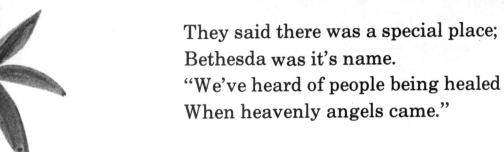

They said there was a special place;
Bethesda was it's name.
"We've heard of people being healed
When heavenly angels came."

"They say that when an angel comes
The water to disturb,
The first one in the pool will be
By heavenly power cured."

New hope had filled their hearts that day.
Their joy was, oh, so great.
They took their son in hopes that God
Their son to walk would make.

So to Jerusalem they went,
Bethesda's pool their aim.
Visions of their son being healed
Made them feel young again.

But they were very much surprised
When to the town they came.
There were so many others there
Whose hopes were all the same.

Each time the angel stirred the pool
The rush was very great.
That by the time they'd reach the pool
They always were too late.

The years went by; in time the man
Found he was all alone.
His parents both were taken to
Their God, their heavenly home.

So now the man was by himself.
His chances now seemed dim.
For when the angel stirred the pool
No one would help him in.

He prayed to God that he might die.
He life no more could bear.
That's when he noticed next to him
The Lord, Christ, standing there.

Then Jesus asked him, "Would you like
To be made well again?"
"I can't, for when I reach the pool
Another's healed by then."

Then Jesus shocked him when He said,
"STAND UP! ROLL UP YOUR MAT."
He felt new strength come to his legs
And stood up just like that.

He stood, he jumped, he walked around;
He thought, *God heard my prayer!*
He turned to Jesus to give thanks,
But Jesus wasn't there.

So he went to the temple
To thank his God above
For showing him such kindness,
For showing him such love.

He was still at the temple
When Jesus met him there,
And Jesus told him, "Sin no more,
Or worse things you may bear."

That's when he knew this was the Lord,
God's very own dear Son.
The One his parents told him of,
This sure must be the One.

He was so very grateful,
He knelt in humble prayer
To thank the Lord for healing him,
For sending Jesus there.

DEAR PARENT

Bethesda was, in today's language, a hospital. The pool of Bethesda was located near the Sheep Gate, where it is likely the sacrificial animals were driven into Jerusalem.

It is characteristic of Jesus' love for His children that He was to be found at the pool of Bethesda. He knew of the man's wretched plight and of his patience with the cross God had given him to bear. After Jesus heard the man's sad answer to His question "Do you want to be healed?" He commanded the man to "rise, take your pallet and walk." Through His divine power, Jesus reversed the course of nature in an instant.

Jesus is just as aware today of our own trials and tribulations. He hears our prayers and answers them according to His wisdom. It is a lesson for us that the man at Bethesda waited 38 years to be cured. How often do we despair and doubt God's providence when we are given a cross to bear for even a fraction of that time.

The apostle Paul, in his letter to the Romans, said: "We know that in everything God works for good with those who love Him" (8:28). Teach your child to trust in Jesus and in His saving grace, for Christ, and only Christ, is "the Way and the Truth and the Life." (John 14:6).

THE EDITOR